Video Marketing Mastery

The Ultimate Video Marketing Strategy Book For Beginners

[O. Addey]

Copyright © 2021 *O. Addey*

All rights reserved.

Table of Contents

Introduction 6
Chapter-01: Why Video Matters for Business 7
    Higher Conversion Rates 7
    Improved Social Reach 8
    Greater Credibility and Trust 9
    Video Marketing Enhances Other Marketing Strategies 9
    Pick an Audience and Set Goals 10
    Maintain Consistent Branding 11
Chapter-02: How to Build a Video Marketing Strategy 12
    Understand your audience and set campaign goals 12
    Keep your brand consistent and your message consistent throughout videos 13
    Make sure your video budget makes sense 13
    Optimize your videos and target them appropriately for each channel 14
        Test and Test again 15
        Engagement rate 15
        View count 16
        Play rate 16

Social Sharing 16

Comments/feedback 17

Don't forget Connected TV ads (CTV) 17

Chapter-03: Choose Between In-House Production or Outsourcing 18

Optimize Videos For Each Platform 18

Track Your Video Success 19

Product Videos 20

Customer Spotlights 20

Small Business Story 21

Chapter-04: How to Make Video Marketing Work for Your Business 22

Create a regular talk show 22

Use live video 23

Give your audience a behind-the-scenes look 24

Make short videos highlighting your employees ... 25

Create a branded web series 25

You Can Do Several Types of Video Marketing 27

    Educational videos 27

    Tutorial videos 27

    Industry update videos 28

    Explainer videos 28

- Company culture videos 28
- Event videos 29
- Brand videos 29
- Product videos 30
- Product launch videos 30
- Testimonial videos 30
- Customer testimonials 31
- Employee testimonials 31

Major types of video marketing 31

Chapter-05: How Do I Create a Video Marketing Strategy? 33

How to Build a Video Marketing Strategy 33

Start with Your Video Goals 34

Determine the Story You Want to Tell 35

What Kind of Video Should I Create? 36

Most Popular Types of Video 36
- Commercials 36
- Social Content Videos 37
- Explainer Videos 37

Conclusion 38

Introduction

The rise of video marketing is a once-in-a-lifetime opportunity for businesses like yours. As customers continue to choose video over other types of information, they want companies of all sizes and industries to interact with them through video. Platforms are progressively favoring video content, and new devices such as phones and tablets are more video ready than ever. That implies that to compete, you must fully utilize this incredible marketing tool. The more time you waste, the more clients you will lose. You're likely to receive a shrug from the ordinary marketer if you question her about her video marketing strategy right now. While most marketers understand the importance of video on a fundamental level – and may even upload files regularly — there isn't necessarily a deeper goal behind it. But there is no denying that video is significant. After all, that is how individuals spend one-third of their time today: viewing internet video content. According to Wyzowl's 2018 Video Marketing Statistics Survey, 81 percent of businesses use video as a marketing technique, up from 63 percent in 2017, and 81 percent of customers have been persuaded to buy a product or service after seeing a brand's video. So, how can you get started with a video marketing plan that would help you achieve more engagement and results?

Chapter-01: Why Video Matters for Business

Video is a powerful medium that enables businesses to engage with their audiences in ways that other forms of media do not. Humans, as visual creatures, have longer attention spans for videos than for text. Despite the potential of video, much small company (SMB) owners believe that video marketing is only available to larger, more established businesses. The cash, time, and expertise required to make videos are the primary reasons small business owners shun this kind of marketing. However, implementing a video marketing plan is considerably easier than you would believe.

Higher Conversion Rates

The ultimate objective of marketing is to convert ordinary viewers into paying customers. According to Vidyard's research from 2015, firms that used video marketing had a 27 percent higher through rate and a 34 percent higher conversion rate than those that did not. Here's what you'll discover:

- Why is video marketing so successful?
- The Advantages of Video Marketing
- What is the best way to create a video marketing strategy?

- What Exactly Is Video Marketing?

Video marketing includes developing, arranging, and distributing videos to promote your company and its products or services to a specific audience. The objective is to keep potential buyers engaged with your business in a fun, approachable, and consumable way. Marketers are well aware that video advertising may produce excellent results. According to HubSpot's 2020 State of Marketing Report, the video was the most popular type of media utilized in content marketing, surpassing blogs and infographics.

- Higher conversion rates
- Benefits of Video Marketing
- Improved social reach
- Enhances other marketing strategies
- Greater credibility and trust

Creating a video marketing plan is more time-consuming than other types of marketing. So before devoting any resources to video creation, consider the advantages of video marketing for the company.

Improved Social Reach

Some of the most popular social networking sites are designed to accommodate visual material. Facebook, Instagram, Pinterest, YouTube, and Twitter provide an excellent opportunity to expand your company's social reach and raise brand recognition. Videos are extremely shareable, and Facebook favors original videos in user feeds. This implies that videos can reach many more people than any other type of advertising post.

Greater Credibility and Trust

Video provides a fantastic chance to establish trust and confidence with your target audience. In an easy-to-digest video format, you may give vital information to potential consumers. You may make the following videos:

- How-to videos
- Instructional videos
- Product descriptions
- Customer spotlights

Videos provide free relevant information to your audience and may establish your company as an expert in your area. In addition, people in your field will be more inclined to come to you first for information or to make a purchase if you are an industry leader.

Video Marketing Enhances Other Marketing Strategies

A video is a dynamic type of marketing that may be used in conjunction with other techniques. For instance, if you're currently producing instructive blogs, you may create the same content in video format to distribute alongside them.

Similarly, if you've amassed a sizable email list, you may begin adding video marketing into your email campaigns to increase their efficacy.

Pick an Audience and Set Goals

Every marketing campaign should start with research. This data helps you target your efforts and enhance the chance of turning them into paying customers. Consider the following questions as you set the basis for an effective video marketing strategy:

- What kind of market do you want to reach?
- What type of material is most sufficient to induce a favorable response from your intended audience?
- Where do they invest most of their time online?
- What do you hope to accomplish with your campaign?

Consider your objectives. Perhaps you want to increase brand awareness by getting your company's name in front of as many people as possible. Maybe you want to introduce a new product by targeting a specific demographic. Clarifying your objectives and comprehending your target audience will provide the groundwork for an effective video marketing approach.

Maintain Consistent Branding

Even if a video marketing strategy is out of character for your organization, you should stick to your core values. This familiarity will appeal to your current audience. New visitors are more likely to interact with your content if they see consistency. Because there are so many moving parts in a video marketing strategy, you may represent your brand through a range of technical characteristics such as:

- Video length
- Script tone and language
- Background music
- Intros and exits
- Camera angles

Attempt to stay on-brand while remaining creative.

Chapter-02: How to Build a Video Marketing Strategy

Understand your audience and set campaign goals

All effective marketing initiatives must begin with research - who are you attempting to reach? What kind of material tend to pique their interest, and where are they most likely to be found? For example, it's pointless to create amazing video content and then pay to have it play on websites that your target audience doesn't frequent.

Most importantly, what objectives are you attempting to achieve with a certain video marketing campaign? Are you attempting to increase brand awareness, sales, traffic, or all of the above? To get the most of the video's potential to connect with your customer, ensure you're utilizing the proper tone of voice and message. Additionally, it is critical to obtain customer insights prior to launching your video since these insights will guide the types of films you make and how much money you will spend on creating them.

Keep your brand consistent and your message consistent throughout videos

While video may appear to be a break from other forms of marketing or a method to try out a branding refresh, people viewing your videos must understand who and what is speaking to them, even if they are startled by the content.

According to McKinsey and Company research, firms with consistent branding outperform those without by 20%. For example, suppose your videos are on YouTube or another social media platform. In that case, they should connect to your website or a landing page with consistent, on-brand content and message across all channels. If the video in your email correspondence differs from the one on Facebook, it is not a consistent portrayal of your brand and may harm rather than assist.

Make sure your video budget makes sense

Many companies make the mistake of assuming that investing a significant amount of money in video creation would ensure its success. But, on the other side, failing to invest adequately in a broad-reaching campaign may undermine your brand's reputation by enabling low-quality messaging to be communicated. So, when it comes to creating the video material, keep your campaign goals in mind and make sure you're spending your money wisely. For example, if you want to attract more millennials or Gen Z customers, you might not need to spend much money on video creation.

Consider creating short films for social platforms like Snapchat, Twitter, and Instagram or repurposing user-generated material. If you have a greater budget and want to keep your brand at the forefront of people's minds, consider creating a fascinating tale in the style of Hollywood (celebs optional). Using influencers in your videos, however, does not always imply enlisting the services of well-known celebrities. To keep costs down, consider incorporating industry experts or even YouTube superstars who already have access to the audience you want to attract, but make sure the individual is well-suited to represent your brand. Investigate their social media accounts, reputation, and the subjects they highlight on their channels and platforms to ensure that they do not damage the ideals of your business or goods.

Optimize your videos and target them appropriately for each channel

According to the channels you choose to launch your advertisements, you'll need to optimize your videos for maximum interaction. This means keeping it brief, posting videos straight to the channel, and adding subtitles to Facebook. For YouTube, this means waiting two weeks after your video is up before making any changes or narrowing your target audience.

And optimizing videos for Twitter requires striking a balance between fine-tuned targeting – from interest to keywords to the device – and not over-targeting to track which campaign is doing the best readily.

Test and Test again

A/B testing, like display ad campaigns, should assist you in figuring out which aspects of a campaign are working and which aren't. Perhaps it's not creative but the messaging, or perhaps it's the time of day you're launching your campaign or the channels you've chosen. Alternatively, your movies may be too long or too short. Whatever it is, make sure you Test, Test and Test again to determine the best content and timing.

Engagement rate

The engagement rate tracks each interaction that a viewer has with your video. For example, how much time did you devote to the video? Did they watch the entire thing, or did they leave early, or did they simply skim through it? This number should indicate the quality of your message, your originality, and if your video is too long or just perfect.

View count

The number of times a video has been viewed is the view count, which varies depending on the channel. For example, on YouTube, a view lasts 30 seconds, but on Facebook, it lasts only 3 seconds. Understanding how people engage with your films across multiple channels means you can improve them. In addition, understanding how each platform counts view count and how to use each platform's insights tools allows you to determine how much actual interaction your video is receiving and allows you to plan future campaigns and content.

Play rate

The number of visitors that pressed the play button to see the video. This is essential since it shows how the video ad performs on certain websites or social media feeds. Maybe it doesn't perform well in the New York Times, but it gets a lot of play on Slate. This reveals information about your target audience. The thumbnail, copy, and even the size of the video may all impact the pay rate.

Social Sharing

This metric counts the number of times your video has been shared on social media networks. People don't bother sharing stuff they don't care about, so if your videos are receiving many shares, it implies your message is getting over.

Comments/feedback

This may appear to be a throwback and not exactly a "metric," but it is a crucial component to consider for any campaign. For example, if viewers leave comments on your social media platforms about your video, read them to determine if they are favorable or bad, and evaluate both. After all, individuals who take the time to view your video and comment, whether they are customers or not, are now familiar with the brand and may become consumers in the future.

Don't forget Connected TV ads (CTV)

People are watching more TV on their mobile devices than ever before. Therefore, CTV advertisements are an excellent method to reach people who spend most of their time. In fact, according to an IAB study, 60% of US marketers expect to transfer their money from linear TV to CTV or OTT in 2021. 1 Consider whether building awareness using CTV advertisements is a suitable fit for your video marketing strategy as you develop it.

Chapter-03: Choose Between In-House Production or Outsourcing

After you have a clear picture of your video marketing campaign's look, it is time to start production. Small business owners are frequently torn between saving money by creating their videos and ensuring quality by engaging a professional crew. While there is no one-size-fits-all approach, there are a few key factors to consider:

- How much money do you have to spend on marketing?
- Your ability to produce in-house
- The level of quality that your target audience expects from you.
- What do local specialists charge?

Both in-house and outsourced video creation have advantages and disadvantages, making it difficult to choose a clear winner. Your company's existing demands and budget will decide the optimal answer.

Optimize Videos For Each Platform

For a video marketing plan, formatting is an often overlooked aspect. Because they are accustomed to seeing movies and television, they film horizontally instinctively. Social networking sites and mobile devices, on the other hand, have generated a need for vertical layouts. Optimizing the structure of your video marketing plan for the platforms on which you advertise can lead to increased interaction and conversion. The landscape style is the most prevalent horizontal format for video marketing on television, PC, and YouTube. However, portrait or vertical formats are perfect for videos you wish to distribute on mobile devices. This format is supported by most social media platforms, including Facebook, Instagram, and Tik Tok.

Track Your Video Success

You must track the results of your video marketing strategy to evaluate its success. Here are some essential metrics to monitor:

- Interaction
- Engagement rate
- View count
- Social sharing

Types of Videos for Your Marketing Strategy

A successful video marketing plan should include a wide range of video genres. The video's objective should determine the perspective, voice, structure, and duration of each video. Let's take a look at some of the most popular marketing videos to get some ideas for your video marketing approach.

Product Videos

Product reviews are perhaps the most frequent and well-known type of video marketing. Businesses now rely significantly on product films to illustrate the value of their goods and services, thanks to the rise of internet purchasing. Customers can receive a far more realistic impression of a product when they see it in movement than static, under ideal lighting circumstances. A product video helps buyers understand the purpose of a product, use it, and why it is helpful. Authentic films also aid in the development of trust between customers and businesses. It ultimately comes down to presenting significance to potential consumers.

Customer Spotlights

Allowing your current customers to speak for you is sometimes the most effective method to express value to new consumers. Online evaluations have been shown to help persuade people to act — but don't stop there. A customer highlight involves one of your customers sharing an amazing story about how your product or service helped them improve their lives.

- This message, when presented in video form, can be beneficial.
- Demonstrate the impact of your company's assistance.
- Describe the efficacy of your products or services.
- Emphasize your brand's image.
- Emphasize the sorts of individuals you serve.

Displaying these testimonials on your website's homepage and social media is a fantastic way to spread the word about your company — and it appears more trustworthy when it comes from someone else.

Small Business Story

Telling your company's narrative is an excellent approach to engage with customers on a more personal level. Clients can perceive the human aspect behind the firm rather than just perceiving you as a cold and dead corporate entity. While it is simple to put up a few lines describing your company's history, video is far more accessible and impactful than a large block of text. Your story film can be as basic as you talking about why you started your business, what you offer customers and your future goals. Tell a tale that only you can tell. A stronger relationship might result in a more devoted client base. Humans, as visual animals, are inherently drawn to and receptive to videos. With an efficient video marketing strategy, you can capture and hold the attention of a large number of potential customers. Check your hosting handle if you wish to post a video to your company's website. Bluehost provides the information and tools to help you. Check out our fantastic web hosting options right now.

Chapter-04: How to Make Video Marketing Work for Your Business

YouTube is used by over a billion people, and individuals spend one-third of their internet time viewing videos.

All of that enthusiasm for video isn't limited to videos created only for pleasure; video marketing also produces amazing results:

- Emails with videos increase clicks by 200 to 300 percent.
- Landing page videos boost conversions by 80%.
- Consumers are 64% more likely to buy a product online after seeing a video.

They may be more expensive to produce than other types of material, but the data show that the investment is well worth it. Of course, like with any sort of material format, there is the risk of oversaturation. If you use video in the same way that every other company in your industry does, you will struggle to stand apart. Here are a few unconventional ways of video marketing that might help you cut through the clutter.

Create a regular talk show

The chat show concept has been around for decades, but companies haven't made much use of it. That implies you'd be the first (or at least one of the first) to tackle this format if you chose to give it a shot. Of course, a talk show format will work best if you commit to doing it regularly, for example, a new episode every month so you can acquire viewers who know when to expect a new episode. And you'll need to put in the effort to research relevant guests and begin building connections with them for them to accept an offer to appear on your program.

The Wine Exchange, a wine boutique in California, interviews winemakers each week in a talk show format to promote different wines and draw attention to their own and guests' businesses. Their YouTube account has thousands of subscribers, and each video they upload has hundreds of views. The films are amusing, instructive, and relevant to the Wine Exchange's target audience: wine buyers. They've made a name for themselves in a crowded field by using the talk show format.

Use live video

With the introduction of Facebook Live, live video on social media has entered the mainstream. It's an excellent method to reach your target audience since everyone who has previously liked your Facebook page will see your video as they go through their feed (and, let's face it, we all know people spend a lot of time reading through their Facebook feeds).

Live video allows you to reply directly to your viewers as they watch, making it more engaging for your audience and useful to you.

Blue Apron's live video showcasing wines that would pair well with Valentine's Day dinners provided an opportunity for the company to address both broad issues of interest to their audiences, such as what to do when ordering wine at a restaurant and particular questions regarding their goods. As a result, they could benefit their audience while also boosting interest in a product they offer. That is the balanced brand that content marketers strive for, and it is one that a smart and well-thought-out live video may help you accomplish.

Give your audience a behind-the-scenes look

Most consumer interactions with a brand occur solely with the final product or via a customer care call or email. You may make your company more genuine and relevant to your prospects by showing them the environment and labor to produce the end product they want.

Most people use Google every day without giving much thought to how the service we rely on operates. If you're curious (and apparently over four million people are), you can watch a film that takes you on a behind-the-scenes tour of the data centers that keep the popular search engine running. Give your consumers a view of what your brand looks like on the inside so they can interact with you on a deeper level. It transforms your brand from an abstract notion to something that people can visualize.

Make short videos highlighting your employees

As much as we hope that all of our marketing will help customers connect with a brand, most individuals find it simpler to connect with other people than with any corporation. Fortunately, your company is made up of individuals. Video allows you to introduce your clients to some of the people behind your company. For example, Freshbooks published a short, humorous video of one of their data analysts, Fernando, completing a Rubik's cube and appealing films that show the Freshbooks workplace and a little bit about the individuals' personality. Both forms of video aid in personalizing the brand and putting a human face to the firm. Videos like this demonstrate to your consumers that their purchase isn't simply benefiting some faceless organization; it's also keeping actual, relatable individuals who (ideally) like their jobs at work.

Create a branded web series

To be honest, this solution is likely to be more expensive than the others described above, but if you can afford it, it might be a wonderful method to generate fresh interest in your business. Several businesses have collaborated with creators to create branded web series that is entertaining enough to pique viewers' interest while also connecting to the company behind them in some manner. For example, GoPro, a business that markets to adventurers, offers a documentary series called Searching the Maya Underworld that follows explorers (who use GoPro cameras) as they dive into a difficult-to-reach cave.

Meanwhile, Nike financed Margot versus Lily, a narrative web series about two sisters who make a bet to launch a new fitness channel. The series is discreet in its brand mentions, yet it is extremely consistent with the subjects that the Nike brand stresses in its advertising. Both of these examples touch on a handful of factors that contribute to the success of branded web series: They must be on issues that are of interest to your target audience.

They should relate to your brand without bombarding your audience with brand references. Branded web series have the potential to be huge if they gain the necessary traction. According to a Contently research, the average number of views for a web series episode is over 200,000 (smaller companies should not depend on such a high number; the median number of views is closer to 3,000).

If you're up for the task, a well-executed branded web series might be an effective method to reach more people and promote your business through video. Suppose you can come up with the proper concept and technique to make a video that captures attention and truly speaks to your target audience. In that case, video can be a great tool for cutting through the noise and encouraging more engagement with your users. Consider carefully including video marketing into your content plan and attempt to go outside the box to provide your audience with something fresh and intriguing.

You Can Do Several Types of Video Marketing

You don't have to be a video content producer specialist to benefit from various forms of video marketing for your organization. For example, making professional films may be as simple as utilizing the camera on your smartphone. Likewise, you don't need high-tech cameras, sophisticated lighting, or a film crew to produce amazing films. Instead, simply focusing on the content in the videos will keep your viewers interested. Here is a list of four distinct forms of video marketing you can perform on your own to help you start making videos like the pros (and some stellar examples of each).

Educational videos

Your viewers will learn something new from educational films. In addition, because you are establishing yourself as an authority in your field, video marketing helps to develop trust between you and your audience. So let's take a look at the many sorts of instructive films you may make for your video marketing strategy.

Tutorial videos

With a tutorial video, you can show off your brand and products while also educating people on utilizing them.

Home Depot performs an excellent job doing this in their video content marketing, describing how to complete DIY projects (such as the wall planter seen below) and demonstrating which of their items are required to complete the task.

Industry update videos

Demonstrating that you monitor and understand market trends will offer you credibility and establish another degree of trust between you and your clients. Whether it's a new technical innovation or a trend that's affecting huge sections of the globe and your sector, this sort of video marketing can keep both you and your consumers up to date. For example, AT&T, the wireless provider, maintains a YouTube playlist dedicated to various industry updates.

Explainer videos

Explainer films are designed to make understanding a product, service, process, or any other difficult issue. These videos are usually animated and don't last more than a few minutes. In the Microsoft example, the firm utilizes animation to demonstrate how its products work together to guard against digital threats.

Company culture videos

Firm culture films serve to showcase the personality of your company. You should shoot videos with your goal and ideals in mind when using this form of video marketing. These films build confidence between your company and the public, especially if you emphasize your devotion to your purpose and values. Culture films are also useful for attracting new employees. People will want to apply if your firm appears to be a wonderful place to work.

Event videos

Without having to say anything, event films may provide a wealth of information about your organization. If your team volunteers together, making a film of your team volunteering might demonstrate how much you care about your neighborhood. If you have a huge work party, you can record how pleased your employees are at your company. If you're organizing a large conference, share speeches or interviews with industry experts who attended the event to create authority and credibility. Apple uses video marketing to promote its events by uploading videos to its YouTube channel in the example below.

Brand videos

Brand video content marketing allows you and your workers to discuss your company's goals and values. Whether you want to convey your firm's commitment to customer experiences or talk about your history, you should utilize your brand film to illustrate what makes your organization special. When developing this type of video marketing, consider why buyers should select your company above the competitors. For example, McDonald's demonstrates their dedication to sustainability with a short promotional film.

Product videos

Product films for your video marketing plan enable you to display your items and pique people's curiosity. Of course, it is up to you how you present your items, but you may also follow in the footsteps of the firms in these instances. Whether the video involves you talking about your product or simply focusing on its features, you want to show off your product's capability. For example, to demonstrate the functions of their coffee machine, Nespresso utilizes a short video with no commentary.

Product launch videos

When it comes to releasing a new product, video marketing may help generate a lot of buzzes. Whether you opt to tease new features in a video marketing campaign or explain the narrative of how your new product came to be, you should aim to make people as thrilled about it as you are. Launch films can be live (as part of a larger event, such as Apple's conferences) or pre-recorded – the option is yours!

Testimonial videos

You demonstrate that customers adore your organization by using testimonials in your video marketing methods. These films, when combined with other content you've generated, aid in the establishment of trust. If people are screaming your praises, your company must be doing well, right? Let's take a look at two distinct kinds of testimonials.

Customer testimonials

Customer testimonials are ideal for moving customers from the contemplation stage of the purchasing process to the purchase stage. For example, if someone compares items from you and a rival and has wonderful client testimonials, they are more inclined to select you. Likewise, Amazon relies on seller testimonials to help build confidence.

Employee testimonials

Your workers understand what it's like to work for you; therefore, they're the ideal individuals to talk about it. With this form of video marketing, job seekers may meet their prospective coworkers. They will get to know the firm better if you include footage of your workplace and activities. LoyaltyOne uses employee testimonials to promote their team and workplaces.

Major types of video marketing

You're ready to start preparing your next video now that you've learned about the many types of video marketing. Here are a few short suggestions for creating outstanding videos:

For shooting, choose a peaceful place. Loud sounds, on the other hand, can spoil an otherwise flawless shot. So unless you're filming an event, you'll want to locate a quiet place to avoid picking up background noises or other people's conversations.

Make the most of natural light.

If you're in a room with windows, make sure the light is in front of you rather than behind you. If the light is excessively strong or casting strange shadows, try changing your position or the curtains if you have any.

When filming a person speaking, keep the camera at eye level.

Awkward shots result from the camera being too high or too low.

When photographing a product, take several close-ups of the product in use.

Close-ups can aid concentrate on certain characteristics, provide context for an explanation, or hide any editing cuts.

Maintain your camera's steadiness.

If you need to buy a tripod for your phone or camera, you may discover several reasonably priced choices online.

Chapter-05: How Do I Create a Video Marketing Strategy?

There is nothing new about video marketing tactics. However, just as you would not produce a commercial and buy airtime during the Super Bowl without first conducting research and strategizing, you should not create a digital marketing video without conducting research and developing a strategy. Your video marketing approach will eventually direct your budget, deadlines, production methods, conversion metrics, and more. As a result, getting this written down and completed should be the first step in your movie-producing process. Before we get into the details, here's a rundown of the steps.

How to Build a Video Marketing Strategy

- Begin with your video objectives.
- Determine your target audience.
- Determine the tale you wish to convey.
- Maintain consistency in your creative requirements.
- Keep to your schedule.
- Maintain a reasonable budget.

Now that you know where we're going let's go into the specifics of each stage.

Start with Your Video Goals

Outlining your film's goals is the first stage in developing your video strategy. However, you must first select which step is the most critical to target.

Awareness: A challenge or opportunity is outlined in this video, and the audience recognizes they have a problem. At this point, your videos should captivate consumers and promote your business to a new audience.

Consideration: The spectator is now thinking about how they will address the situation. They're doing research, asking for advice, reading product reviews, and looking for the most cost-effective solutions.

Decision: The answer is almost there, and you want to be at the forefront of people's minds. Provide proof of client happiness to your prospect and demonstrate why your product or service should be selected above the competition.

You should develop an awareness stage video if you want to attract new clients to your company. A contemplation stage video will help you engage your audience. If you're nearing the end of a transaction and need to nurture your prospects, make a decision stage video. You may also make a video to thank people who have previously purchased from you, as well as an internal film to inspire your staff or attract new personnel.

Determine the Story You Want to Tell

Choosing the tale you want your movie to convey may be both the most enjoyable and the most challenging aspect. But, first, you should sketch out the four elements listed below.

Protagonist with a goal – This individual should fit into your target demographic.

Conflict – This is your customer's problem.

Quest – This is how your product or service will be introduced.

Resolution – This is how your product or service solves the problem.

These components of your tale should lead the viewer on a trip consistent with your brand's goal. As you write your narrative, consider what emotions you want it to evoke in the reader. You want them to laugh, don't you? Should your video make them feel motivated or happy? Consider what feeling you want your audience to feel while you create your script. Everything from the objects and setting to the colors and clothing will express this, so select each element carefully! These components of your tale should lead the viewer on a trip consistent with your brand's goal.

What Kind of Video Should I Create?

After you've developed your approach, it's time to consider the actual video you'll make. Isn't it simple? No, not quite...

Every type and style of video has advantages and disadvantages. Some sorts may be better for you based on your unique marketing goals, while others may be better if you're just seeking to save money in the long run.

You're not alone if you don't know the difference. That's why we've broken down some of the most popular types and styles of the video so that you can get started on your video production!

Most Popular Types of Video

Commercials

They're the most popular sort of video, and you've undoubtedly seen a lot of them on TV, streaming services, or video platforms like YouTube. Commercials are generally wide in appeal and give just the most critical and relevant information a viewer could require because their primary purpose is to acquire new consumers. They're also, most crucially, memorable! They showcase your brand in a way that remains with the viewer, so even if it's the viewer's first exposure to your business, they won't forget it.

Commercials are generally 30 seconds to one minute long and delivered through paid advertising online or on television. They're also ideal for your website or homepage since they give a basic overview of your company and embody your brand purpose in a concise and easy-to-digest style.

Social Content Videos

Short video snippets made specifically for social networking sites such as Facebook, Instagram, Twitter, Linked In, etc. These are generally entertaining, lively, and engaging, and they are meant to be shared. They might contain lifestyle shots, a montage of scenes about your product or service, sound clips or quotations from interviews, or just a stunning image of your goods. Try to keep your social media content films around 30 seconds long. Pay attention to features specific to social media, such as muted autoplay and video looping; you may utilize these tools to your advantage by experimenting with quiet music and generating infinite cycles. Also, use social media to showcase excellent customer comments – this enhances your reputation and spreads positive word of mouth.

Explainer Videos

Educate your audience on your organization, brand, product, or service. Almost any video, like social content videos, maybe an explainer video; the only criteria focus on how your firm addresses a specific problem. Explainer videos are fantastic ways to introduce your brand. They should be able to describe what your firm does and why it is important in a short period. Explainers are typically three minutes long and conclude with a powerful call to action and a straightforward solution to a complicated problem.

Conclusion

How can you make the most of the footage you already have? Can you make a more forceful call to action? Is it possible for you to distribute it on another platform? Consider how you might expand the reach and impact of your video. If you want to gain additional visibility, consider posting your video on a new channel. If your click-throughs or conversions are underwhelming, investigate if you can add an end card with a larger CTA, change the description content, or offer an incentive for clicking through, such as a limited-time discount or a contest. Your video clip can also be re-edited. Viewers lose interest fast if your view-through rates are low. Make a shorter version of your video that will be more appealing to your viewers. To liven up the material, you might try adding visuals. Although you don't want to completely alter your original video, making many versions of it may yield better results. You should also utilize your data and insights to fine-tune your future video approach. View-through rate should influence video duration, and audience demographics should influence your video's content, characters, and voice-over. The most effective distribution channels should influence where to focus distribution efforts. Use this data to develop a more thorough approach the next time so that any future marketing videos you make are successful.

www.ingramcontent.com/pod-product-compliance
Lightning Source LLC
Chambersburg PA
CBHW030039230526
45472CB00002B/590